THE MAGIC OF WILLPOWER

Boost the Power of Resoluteness and Self-control in Your Life

A Happy Thoughts Initiative

THE MAGIC OF WILLPOWER
By WOW Publishings Pvt. Ltd.

Copyright © WOW Publishings Pvt. Ltd.
All Rights Reserved 2024

ISBN : 978-81-947801-0-6

Published by WOW Publishings Pvt. Ltd., India

First edition published in September 2020
First Reprint published in February 2025

Printed and bound by Trinity Academy For Corporate Training Ltd, Pune

Based on the Hindi book titled "Icchashakti Ka Chamatkaar"
by **Sirshree** Tejparkhi

Copyright and publishing rights are vested exclusively with WOW Publishings Pvt. Ltd. This book is sold subject to the condition that it shall not by way of trade or otherwise, be lent, resold, hired out, or otherwise circulated without the publisher's prior written consent in any form of binding or cover other than that in which it is published and without a similar condition including this condition being imposed on the subsequent purchaser and without limiting the rights under copyright reserved above, no part of this publication may be reproduced, stored in or introduced into a retrieval system, or transmitted, in any form, or by any means, electronic, mechanical, photocopying, recording or otherwise, without the prior written permission of both the copyright owner and the above-mentioned publisher of this book. Any person who does any unauthorized act in relation to this publication may be liable to criminal prosecution and civil claims for damages.

Although the author and publisher have made every effort to ensure accuracy of content in this book, they hereby disclaim any liability to any party for any loss, damage, or disruption caused by errors or omissions, resulting from negligence, accident, or any other cause. Readers are advised to take full responsibility to exercise discretion in understanding and applying the content of this book.

Editor's Note

1. This book comprises of two parts. Part 1 provides various techniques to regain your self-control. Part 2 deals with ways of increasing your willpower.

2. Every chapter ends with a sample table that can be used to introspect how you will apply the particular technique of the chapter in your context.

Contents

	Preface	7
	PART 1 - TECHNIQUES TO DEVELOP SELF-CONTROL	**11**
1.	Controlling the Senses	13
2.	Control over Trivial Things	17
3.	Overcoming Emotional Reactions	20
4.	Freedom from Addictions and Bad Habits	24
5.	Control over Food Intake	28
6.	Control over Anger and Annoyance	32
	PART 2 - WILLPOWER	**37**
7.	Relentless Willpower	39
8.	Break Lazy Habits	42
9.	Strengthening Willpower	46
10.	Boost your Willpower to Live	49
11.	Augmenting Willpower	52

PREFACE
WILLPOWER AND SELF CONTROL

Man is full of various desires. As soon as one desire is fulfilled, he strives to fulfill the next one. One after the other, wishes keep popping up, either by looking at incidents or people around him. But, only those wishes that are infused with an inner strength get fulfilled. This inner strength is known as **Willpower.**

Without this inner strength, many times, we are unable to accomplish some of the essential tasks, even if we desire to do so. Here's an example: a student wants to study more but fails to do so more often because of various distractions. Some more common examples are waking up early, choosing the right words while talking, maintaining ideal body weight, acquiring one's aim, etc. To fulfill such desires, we need to increase our willpower. Only then will we be able to fulfill our dreams.

There were two bright students in a class. They excelled in studies but lagged in sports. One day, the schoolteacher announced an award to the students who would excel in sports. Both those students wished to be recognized in sports as well. Hence, they enrolled themselves in the sports activity. But, as they started practicing, each one had a different stream of thoughts running in his mind.

One of the students thought, "I'll be glad if I win this competition… With studies, now I will excel in sports too, my parents will be proud of me, and so on." The more he thought about it, the more his willpower rose, making his resolution to excel more firm.

On the other hand, the other student's thoughts were exactly the opposite. He felt, "What if I lose? What will people say? My family members will be disappointed with me. I will lose my confidence, etc." Negative thoughts like these weakened his desire to compete. He thought of running away and ultimately withdrew from the competition.

From the above example, we understand how one student was inspired to take part in sports, whereas the other lost his will. By giving the right direction to thoughts, we can increase our willpower. This, in turn, will help us achieve our desires.

When people want to achieve success, health, learn some art, or develop some quality within, they should be able to kindle their willpower. For this, asking questions, such as: "What will I gain by fulfilling this desire? How happy will I feel?" will inspire us to strive more. It gives the required strength to achieve the aim.

The magic of willpower not only helps us to achieve what we desire but also helps us to control undesirable habits like excessive eating, bad habits, addictions, anger, and many more. These unwanted habits are a roadblock in attaining success. One needs to practice self-control to change these habits. But to bring this *self-control*, one needs to have that inner strength— willpower.

When one wants to get rid of unwanted habits and addictions, one should be able to channel thoughts in the right direction. One should think about the harmful effects of the addiction like how it can sicken them, how it will lead to suffering, how it will increase their medical expenses, how it will amount to misuse of money, how it will feel when people make fun of this habit, etc. This kind of contemplation and visualization of the truth can help achieve self-control as well as boost willpower, which then leads to achieving desired results.

Don't we always wish to be mentally strong and trustworthy? But for this, our words and actions need to be aligned. We need to deliver what we have committed. This is possible with the help of strong willpower. When our willpower is weak, we tend to brag a lot without following it up with appropriate action. What we say, should be aligned with what we do. This makes us mentally strong, reliable, and trustworthy.

Weak willpower further leads to loss of respect for oneself. Hence one should strengthen willpower to safeguard one's self-esteem. In this book, we will not only learn to give the right direction to our willpower but understand techniques that will help us get rid of unwanted habits and strengthen our willpower. If applied fully, it will increase mental strength. No stress or challenge can then control us. We will be able to achieve whatever we wish to. We will find harmony and balance in whatever we do.

PART 1
TECHNIQUES TO DEVELOP SELF-CONTROL

1

CONTROLLING THE SENSES
THE 'NO' GESTURE TECHNIQUE

One day, two friends were strolling in a village. They saw a herdsman leading his cow with a rope around its neck. On watching this, one of the friends asked the other, "Tell me, who is tied to whom?"

"What kind of silly question is that? How can a herdsman ever be tied to a cow? It's obvious the rope is around the cow's neck, and the herdsman is holding it," replied the other friend with a laugh.

The friend again asked, "Say, if the cow were to free itself from its rope and run away, what would the herdsman do?"

"Of course, he would run after the cow!"

"And what if the herdsman escapes? What will the cow do?"

"The cow would escape as well!" was his instant reply.

"Now tell me, who's *actually* tied to whom?"

After listening to this question, the friend was silent, and it set him thinking. "Yes, that's right. It's a delusion. We think that it's the cow that is bound, but in reality, it's the herdsman who is bound."

When a person contemplates deeply, he is then able to understand the difference between reality and delusion.

Just as the herdsman is tied to the cow and not the other way around, similarly, man is tied to his mind and senses. He is deluded and thinks that he is guiding his senses. But in reality, it's the opposite. The senses keep pulling him to fulfill their desires. Conclusively, the senses control a person.

Till the end of his life, man's senses keep demanding fulfillment. Senses trap him. It's only when he becomes old that his senses begin to weaken, leading to poor eyesight, reduced listening capacity, loss of appetite, memory loss, etc. But till then, the senses continue with their demands for satiation. The mind, too, keeps generating new desires.

The actual aim of human life is to free itself of this excessive indulgence in satisfying the senses. Hence, we must train our senses with the help of self-control.

Let us understand this with the help of an example. A student is writing his examination. But his pen refuses to write anything. Now, despite knowing all the answers, he is unable to write anything. As a result, he fails.

Similarly, we will not be able to attain complete success if our senses, like the student's pen, are untrained and lack self-control. They won't cooperate with us when we need them the most.

Trained senses are essential to lead a successful and efficient life. Some people train their bodies in such a way that they can sit comfortably in any posture. This helps in maintaining good health in the long run. Likewise, trained senses yield positive results.

Let us now understand how to liberate oneself from this over-indulgence in the senses.

Let's use a hand gesture: **Lift both your hands. Now bend them at the elbows and move them back towards your shoulders, just as you would say an emphatic 'NO' to someone.** This gesture is the sign of freedom from sense-gratification.

One can use this gesture to invoke their willpower and gain self-control. With this gesture, it is as if you are saying, "I am not going to indulge in this. I have nothing to do with this."

This hand gesture works as an anchor—a means of giving a new message to the brain. The body and mind function according to the command passed by the brain.

Let's understand this with another example. Whenever we join our hands in prayer, what do we experience? We automatically experience a peaceful and divine feeling within. Keep aside this book for a moment and close your eyes. Now join your hands together as you would while you pray. The feeling of devotion and surrender will automatically arise within you.

This happens because the brain is already programmed. There is a link established between the joining of hands and prayer since childhood. Whenever the brain associates a hand gesture with a particular feeling, then the same sentiments are triggered every time we use that gesture.

Likewise, when this 'NO' hand gesture gets programmed in the brain, the message is relayed to the brain to stop indulging in the senses. This helps to overpower the demand of the senses.

Use this gesture initially for small things repeatedly. Example: When your tongue says "eat more," then you can use it to convey a 'NO.' The senses will try to accomplish things based on old habits, but it helps to remember that we are now aiming to train our senses.

Hence when the eyes want to indulge in a wrong scene, say 'NO' using the gesture. When the ears want to listen to others' criticism, use the same gesture.

In this way, whenever the mind wants to indulge in undesirable things, use this gesture to achieve self-control.

Create a Contemplation Chart to practice self-control. Below is an example chart for your reference. You may create a similar table for yourself based on your habits.

\multicolumn{4}{c}{**Contemplation Chart**}			
Senses	**Events which ensnare the senses**	**Negative effect**	**A positive effect of saying 'No.'**
Eyes	Watching movies indiscriminately.	Other tasks suffer due to insufficient time	Accomplishing tasks on time
Ears	Listening to music late into the night.	Inadequate sleep and fatigue.	Keeping fresh all-day.
Tongue			
Nose			
Skin			

2
CONTROL OVER TRIVIAL THINGS
THE DELAYED GRATIFICATION TECHNIQUE

In the United States, a well-known experiment was carried out on children aged 7 to 9 years. Two pieces of marshmallows were placed in front of the children. They were told, "If you want to eat it right away, then you shall receive only one marshmallow. But if you wait for twenty minutes, you will get two."

Three types of responses were observed at the end of the experiment. The children were categorized into three groups based on these responses.

The first group said, *"We want to eat the marshmallow right now. We can't wait,"* and they ate it immediately.

The second group said, *"We shall wait for twenty minutes."* During this period, they touched the marshmallow, smelled it, and looked at it from all angles. They spent their time concentrating on the marshmallow. But they did manage to keep themselves in check.

The children of the third group distracted themselves away from the marshmallow. They engaged themselves in other activities and kept themselves occupied for those twenty minutes.

Years later, the life of all the children from the three groups was observed. The observation concluded that some children from the first group were not as mature and successful as children from the second and third groups. The children from the second and third groups used the habit of Delayed Gratification to have more control over themselves. This quality helped them achieve more significant successes easily.

Right from a young age, children should be trained to increase their willpower by exercising their self-control. This will help them move ahead in life smoothly.

Most of the decisions that many of us take today are perhaps like the children of the first group. New technology and the need for instant gratification are destroying our patience. We want instant results for everything—food delivery, sightseeing, shopping, etc. Advertisements today state, "Call us for immediate dispatch. It will be express delivered at your place," etc. "You want to enjoy our Pizza; it shall reach you within 20 minutes. If we're late, it will be free!"

Fulfillment first and payment later is the slogan of increasingly more advertisements today. You don't have to stand in a queue. The moment a desire arises in a person's mind, companies out there are ready to fulfill it. As a result, the quality of Delayed Gratification is becoming a rare virtue.

Let's understand what this quality is and how to develop this quality to achieve the desired results in life.

Delayed Gratification means **deliberately waiting for some time before completing any desire.**

For instance, a teenager would be asked to wait for some time before answering the phone or to wait for a couple of minutes before playing a game or listening to music. This does not mean that one should stop using the mobile phone; instead, delay its use for some time.

The quality of Delayed Gratification can increase your willpower and self-control only when you deliberately hold back your compulsion or temptation for a couple of minutes. But most people equate such waiting to being deprived of their happiness of using their mobile phone. The mobile phone has become a compulsive necessity today.

We should use this quality in daily life situations to nurture it. For instance, if you are going to have your food, wait for some time before eating. If you are going to answer the phone, let it ring three to four times before answering. Similarly, if you want to check your messages or download videos, wait for some time before doing it. In this manner, using common sense wherever possible, wait for a little time before engaging in a task. This technique will help to develop willpower by using self-control.

If you have trouble waiting, you can counter it by completing a small task during your wait period. You may choose some other tasks like sending an email, doing a 2-minute workout, or tidying your place. Small activities like these can help you in the practice of Delayed Gratification. Stop for a little time before using conveniences.

You can create a contemplation chart and identify activities or tasks which you will consciously delay as a practice of delayed gratification. Here's an example:

Contemplation Chart				
No.	Which desires are you in a hurry to complete	Wait- time	Delay benefits
1.	Buying a new mobile phone.	One month	Saving money. Spending on essentials.

3

OVERCOMING EMOTIONAL REACTIONS
THE WHEN-THEN TECHNIQUE

There is a popular folk story of a Brahmin and his wife, who used to stay in a village. The wife was unhappy as they were childless. One day, the Brahmin got a baby mongoose to cheer her up. Gradually, she shifted to a happy mindset, entertained by the mongoose's presence.

Time passed, and the Brahmin's wife was now expecting. Soon she gave birth to a healthy baby. As she got busy with her baby, she slowly started ignoring the mongoose.

One day, she went out for some work, leaving the baby in the crib. A while later, a snake entered the baby's room. As it got closer to the crib, the mongoose detected the snake. The mongoose immediately attacked and killed the snake.

Glad and proud that it had saved the baby, the mongoose thought the Brahmin's wife would now shower him with love and appreciation. He came out of the house and waited for her in eager anticipation.

As the Brahmin's wife neared the house, she saw the mongoose at the door. Blood was smeared all over his mouth. Seeing this ghastly sight, she feared and concluded that the mongoose had killed her baby. In a fit of rage, she lifted a big stone and crushed the mongoose. She then ran inside the house towards the crib.

To her surprise, she found the baby safe and sound in the crib, but a snake was lying dead nearby. Looking at the scene, she now understood what had transpired. The mongoose had saved the baby's life. The sight filled her with remorse. But now, she had to live with this guilt for the rest of her life.

Looking at the mongoose's mouth smeared with blood, the Brahmin's wife had spun a wrong story in her mind. She couldn't control her emotional outburst. Without understanding the real truth, she had killed the innocent mongoose. If only she had more self-control and patience, she would have examined what had exactly happened. She wouldn't have to regret the deed for the rest of her life.

In many such incidents, we lose self-control and react out of compulsion, bringing life-long guilt and resentment.

We have often observed that trivial arguments in families lead to bigger fights later on. This is because the mind jumps to conclusions and spins stories, leading to a loss of self-control.

We tend to lose self-control because we lack the willpower to direct our feelings and get overtly attached to our negative emotions. We either have an outburst of emotions or suppress them.

Let us understand this in detail.

When people face adverse incidents or receive criticism, some respond with an emotional outburst. They lose self-control and react by using abusive language. Others suppress their emotions as they find it difficult to express themselves. Deep within, they experience suffocation of emotions.

But for our betterment, both should be avoided—*emotional outbursts* and *suppression of emotions*. Instead, we should use our willpower and regulate our reactions. This helps in developing emotional maturity. We can use the **When-Then** technique to control our emotions. This technique comes handy during an outburst of emotions like anger, jealousy, greed, hatred, or revenge.

The When-Then technique involves contemplating *much before* one becomes the victim of an emotional outburst.

Here are some examples.

"**When** I feel angry, what will I do?" "**Then** I will be a witness to the sensations of anger in my body and will either count backward from 100 to 1 or drink cold water. I will take 2 to 3 deep breaths, or will remind myself that I will not punish myself for others' mistakes, etc."

"**When** I feel like mocking or abusing someone, **then** I will laugh and postpone this urge, or will try to move away from that situation, or will try to remember the other person's virtues."

"**When** I feel hatred or vengeful at someone, **then** I will divert my attention to some other activity, or I will examine this feeling and contemplate its futility."

Thus, the *When-Then* technique can be creatively used in various situations. We can create a table of what we will specifically do when negative emotions like greed, boredom, etc., assail us. If we have prepared such a table, we might probably remember something from this table in the midst of testing situations.

This technique will help in raising our awareness. When we receive a negative response, this technique will help us exercise self-control in those situations. It will help in boosting our confidence, which in turn will increase our willpower.

Contemplation Chart		
Emotions	When do they arise?	What will you do?
Anger	Tea is not served on time	I will focus on my breathing or will try to imagine the taste of tea while happily waiting for tea to be served.
Greed		
Fear		
Worry		
Others.		

4

FREEDOM FROM ADDICTIONS AND BAD HABITS
THE ART OF SAYING 'NO'

Harish was a young guy who had taken to the habit of gambling. His family members were distressed due to this habit of his. They counseled him to leave this habit, but all in vain. Whenever they asked him to reform himself, his response was, "I am not into this habit; instead, the habit is holding me." He genuinely wanted to get rid of the habit but was unsuccessful despite many attempts.

As a solution to his problem, his family got him married to Asha. Initially, things were going well between Harish and Asha. But after a few months, he picked his gambling habit again. Asha was now worried too. She made a determined decision to help him get rid of this habit.

One day, Asha got to know about a spiritual master. She and Harish visited him at his Ashram. Asha shared her problems with the master. Listening to her, the master understood the root of the problem and asked them to re-visit the next day.

When they visited the Ashram the next day, they found the master holding onto a tree.

Perplexed, they asked him, "What are you doing? Why are you holding onto the tree in this manner?"

He said, "Please leave and return tomorrow."

They visited the next day and found the master in the same position.

Harish asked, "Master, what are you doing?"

"This tree is not leaving me, so please visit me again tomorrow."

Harish lost his patience and asked anxiously, "O Great Sage, what are you saying? Why don't you leave this tree?"

"What can I do, the tree is not leaving me?"

He laughed, "*You* are holding onto the tree; the tree is not holding you. You can leave the tree whenever you desire."

"This is exactly what I am trying to tell you from the past couple of days. *You* are holding on to the habit of gambling; the habit is not holding you. So, you can leave this habit whenever you decide," said the master as he walked away from the tree.

Harish realized his mistake. He understood that he alone was responsible for his bad habits. If one desires, they can examine their habit with awareness, understand its demerits, and quit the habit with the help of willpower.

It is rightly said: Man first makes habits; later, habits make the man. We need to apply this proverb in our life. Otherwise, we become slave to our bad habits, and we don't realize this until they have become addictions.

Whenever we hear the word "addiction," what comes to our mind is—alcohol, tobacco, cigarettes. But besides these, many other addictions have trapped us, such as binge-watching, consuming copious amounts of tea or coffee, wasteful shopping, playing games on the mobile, checking WhatsApp, excessive chatting on the Social Media, gossiping, etc. We do not consider these habits as addictions, and hence the thought of getting rid of them never crosses our mind.

A 35-year-old lady harbored immense fear for diseases. She would consume medicines for every little ailment. Despite knowing the side-effects of overdosing, she could not stop herself from popping pills every day. Due to this habit, the level of toxins in her body rose. Her health deteriorated even further, and she kept increasing her dose of medicines. Soon this habit led to her death. An unsuspected habit can also assume life-threatening proportions.

Nowadays, there are de-addiction centers around the world to help people get rid of their addictions. But awareness needs to be generated for smaller addictions and habits first. Working towards removing those habits can be done as soon as possible before it becomes an obsession.

It is important to raise our willpower to gain self-control. But our habits are such that they overpower our willpower. Hence, we need to learn the habit of saying "NO" from today onwards.

Generally, we find it difficult to refuse when someone offers us tea insistently. In such situations, we will have to learn the habit of saying "NO" outright. Whenever we get this opportunity, we should be able to say "NO." However, it might be quite challenging for some people to say, "NO." "What will the other person think about me? How can I say No?" Such thoughts compel us to lose control. Hence our refusal should be so firm that the other person would not think of repeating the offer.

People who find it difficult to say "NO" should look in the mirror and practice saying "NO" at least ten times daily. Slowly extend this practice to include family members, friends, and other acquaintances.

Finally, one should develop this habit with oneself. Even if there is no one around, or you are alone, you should be able to control yourself. You should be able to tell yourself clearly, "I am not going to do this; instead, I am going to invest my time in some good work."

In this manner, you can start saying "NO" in trivial incidents. It will help in developing self-control. As against this, start saying "YES" to whatever good habits you want to inculcate. This habit will prepare you for developing good habits in the future.

Create a Contemplation Chart that will help you inculcate better habits for a successful future

Habits to say "NO" to	Habits to say "YES" to	Habits to be continued
Laziness	Daily exercise	Sleeping early
Consuming an extra cup of tea	Writing a Diary	Keeping things in their appointed places.

5

CONTROL OVER FOOD INTAKE
THE DISSIPATION TECHNIQUE

There was a wealthy man who was obese and used to fall sick quite often. The main reason for his deteriorating health was his habit of food binging. He had no control over his food eating habits. He loved tasting various delicacies and kept eating throughout the day. He had a sedentary job; hence there was a lack of physical exercise as well.

Once, he developed a bad cough. He visited an Ayurvedic physician for treatment. The physician gave him medicines and asked him to avoid eating tangy (sour) foods for a while.

After a week, he revisited the physician with the same complaint as there was no improvement in his condition.

"The medicines should have cured your cough. Did you eat any tangy or cold food that you were supposed to refrain from?"

The rich man sheepishly accepted that he liked tangy food like pickles, curds, etc., and hence couldn't control himself from eating them.

"Now, you may eat whatever you want to; it will lead to three benefits."

"Benefits! What are they?"

The physician answered, "First benefit – you will never be robbed. Second benefit – you will never be bitten by a dog. Third benefit – you will never be old."

Perplexed by the physician's answer, the man asked, "Are you joking? Please explain."

"If you continue to eat tangy or sour food, you are never going to recover from your cough. Listening to your cough, a thief will think that you are wide awake and hence will never think of robbing your house.

"The second benefit – a dog will never bite you because you will become weak due to your illness. Hence you will need a stick to walk around. Seeing a stick in your hand, no dog will come close to you.

"The last benefit – Due to your illness and weakness, you will soon be dead. Hence you will not have to bear the sufferings of old age."

The rich man understood the serious hints given by the physician. He then diligently practiced control over his eating habits, and within a few days, he was able to get rid of his cough and regain his health.

From the above story, it becomes clear that **once the adverse effects of our actions or habits becomes visible, our self-control automatically begins to grow.**

Eating habits play a crucial role in one's life. In olden times, people used to eat food as a means to survive and ate only as much as they needed.

But in today's modern times, it is not a need anymore; instead, food has become a desire. Variety and taste have taken precedence over a nutritious and healthy meal.

You may have heard people making comments like, "Have you tried this cuisine," "This particular dish at that restaurant is delicious. You must try it," "If you visit that city but don't taste the sweets and snacks it's famous for, then your trip is a waste," etc.

Eating street food that's fried, unhygienic, and unhealthy, gives rise to various diseases. Today, *people are not just consuming food; instead, food is consuming them!* We need to understand the depth of this sentence and keep a check on our food habits.

We need to eat food with awareness. Food consumed with awareness reminds us of our stomach's capacity to digest. Hence, we can consume accordingly. Food consumed in non-awareness does not impart a sense of fulfillment. We also need to check whether we are eating for the betterment of our health or just to satisfy our taste buds.

But even after knowing the repercussions, there are times when we tend to overeat or crave to eat inappropriate or unhealthy food. At such times, we can apply the **Dissipation technique** to achieve self-control.

This technique helps us overcome the feeling of dissatisfaction due to food. We can dissipate foods that are harmful to our health. Hence it is called the Dissipation technique.

Let us understand this technique with some examples.

Suppose a person loves eating chocolates. Hearing the word "chocolate" is enough to make his mouth water. A glimpse of the chocolate bar, its taste, and smell is enough to melt away his self-control. He can feel and smell the taste of chocolate immediately. He cannot hold himself back from binging on chocolates. But as he has diabetes, he wants to break this habit. The dissipation technique comes handy in such situations. Let's read how.

In this technique, he has to imagine that the chocolate is made of wood straw. Hence, it tastes like wood. So, he visualizes that instead of chocolate, he is chewing a piece of wood.

When one uses his imagination in such a way, the craving to eat chocolate automatically reduces. This is because he dissipated the taste of chocolate and replaced it with an undesirable taste. But he needs to use this imagination time and again so that this image gets anchored in his brain. Later, the brain automatically works on its own.

You can use this technique for those foods which are harmful to your health, and which you can't stop yourself from having.

Apart from food, this technique is useful for getting rid of other addictions as well. Say someone is addicted to smoking. He feels relaxed after having a smoke. Using this technique, he can imagine that he feels discomforted and restless after smoking. He can also visualize that his lungs and liver are in a jail made of the physical body and are crying out for help, "Stop... stop smoking." One can also imagine that the cigarette is made of kerosene or the burnt rubber tube of a tyre that emanates a strong stench after being lit—a stench that he cannot tolerate. With this, he will now have a newfound awareness before smoking. By using this visualization over and over again, there is a strong chance that he remembers the smell the next time he picks up a cigarette. Otherwise, an addicted person has little or no realization before picking up a cigarette or alcohol.

The important aspect of this technique is to imagine illogical and impossible things like chocolate-made-of-wood-straw or a cigarette-made-of-burnt-rubber-tube.

The Dissipation technique can help you overcome all the bad habits that you find challenging today. This faith will ultimately help you conquer your temptations.

Create a contemplation chart as shown below and start applying this technique to get rid of those unwanted habits or addictions.

Contemplation Chart		
No.	Habit	Dissipation Technique
1	Excessive Coffee	Imagine a tangy flavor in coffee

6

CONTROL OVER ANGER AND ANNOYANCE
THE DELAYED REACTION MEDITATION

Incidents that occur beyond our control or against our wish generate anger within us. Anger is an emotion where a person punishes himself for other people's mistakes by being upset and bothered. He suffers because he is unable to control his anger. Hence, if we treasure our happiness and peace, we need to learn to control our anger.

Most people are often victims of anger. They generally blame other people or situations for their state. But they fail to understand that anger was already lying dormant within them; people and situations were just a trigger to let it out.

Let us understand this with an example:

There were two students whose final exam results out. The first student had failed his exam while the second secured 89%. Both went home with their results.

The first student's father was ecstatic as he got promoted at his job that day. When he heard about his son's failure, he didn't react much as he was in a happy state.

The second student's father was upset with his son's results. He felt his son could have scored 90% if he would have just worked a bit harder. He shouted at his son for scoring 1% lesser marks.

From the above story, it becomes clear that situations outside do not govern a person's anger; instead, it is dependent on his mood; it arises from the inner state of the person. If a person is in a good mood, then he is capable of forgiving even a big mistake. But, in a bad mood, even a small mistake is enough to set the person off.

Hence more than improving the situations outside, we need to work on our mood and the anger burning within.

People often ask this question, "What to do when we are angry?" Well, the answer is – **Nothing can be done when you are angry. Whatever needs to be done should be worked out much earlier, well before anger sets in.**

The Delayed reaction meditation is one of the best ways of controlling anger. In this meditation, you learn to delay the urge to react immediately, for a while.

If we practice the Delayed Reaction meditation, then there is a possibility that we can exercise self-control in situations that create anger within us and can procrastinate our reaction.

Delayed Reaction means whenever we want to react to a situation, delay that reaction a little. When we experience discomfort, the mind immediately wants to take care and starts giving instructions to the body to move. If we feel itchy, we want to scratch immediately; if we feel hot, we instantly switch on the fan. Such reactions happen because we do not want to bear any inconvenience or feel any discomfort, even for a moment.

Anger too causes inconvenience within us, and hence we blast out without even understanding its ill-effects and then suffer. To stop this reaction, let us understand how to practice this Delayed Reaction meditation.

Let us first read and understand it fully, and then practice this meditation:

1. Set a timer on your mobile or watch for 15 to 20 minutes (you may begin with 5 to 10 minutes as well).
2. Close your eyes and sit in a comfortable posture for meditation.

3. Take 2 to 3 deep breaths and release slowly.
4. Concentrate on your breaths during the entire meditation.
5. While in meditation, whenever you feel the urge to open your eyes, move your hands, straighten your clothes, or stretch your legs, tell yourself, "Delay the Reaction—let me wait for a while before reacting."
6. In between, you can tell yourself "No Reaction" during the meditation. You may like or dislike certain things but do not react. In case you do react, then there should be "No Reaction" to that action as well.

    Similarly, even if you are experiencing confusion in your thoughts or experiencing a state of no thoughts, there should be "No Reaction." There is no need to unravel or tackle anything. Just experience the confused or thoughtless state as it is.
7. In the same way, tell yourself "No Reaction" for every thought that arises. Thoughts will automatically reach their natural end. There is no need to DO anything. Even if you are unable to control your thoughts, "No Reaction." Continue meditating in this manner.
8. After meditating with the conviction of "No Reaction" for 15 to 20 minutes, slowly open your eyes.

This meditation serves as an opportunity to break the old habit of instant reaction. You can try experimenting with this in various ways. The learning experienced in this meditation will free you from all negative reactions.

Create a chart for contemplation on the various situations that anger you and how 'No Reaction' can benefit. An example is given below.

Situations that cause wrong response	Effect	What to do next?
When someone says something negative, we immediately get angry and start retorting. We copy the behavior of the other person and react in the same way.	Strained Relationships	Offering No Reaction, will maintain peace and generate good feelings for the other person in our mind.

PART 2
WILLPOWER

7

RELENTLESS WILLPOWER
THE HALLMARK OF SUCCESS

One needs several qualities to be successful in life. Amongst them, *relentless willpower* is one of the essential attributes. History is replete with examples where people did not have access to conveniences, facilities, or luxuries, and yet they could achieve their goals with the help of their relentless willpower.

Christopher Columbus—the great voyager—had an acute desire to cross the Atlantic Ocean to find a new course to the East. During the voyage, his sailors lost courage and revolted. But he remained steadfast in his resolve and ultimately crossed the Atlantic ocean to discover the American continent.

Many great people, due to their steadfast and tenacious willpower, persevered when others declared their goals to be impossible or ridiculed them.

Mahatma Gandhi's willpower was so unswerving that the British monarchy had to leave India.

It is rightly said, "**Relentless willpower is the key to success.**" The spirit of relentless willpower is imbued in the statement, **"Come what may; I will accomplish this task!"**

But many people find it challenging to complete their tasks, as small obstacles prevent them from progressing further. This indicates a lack of willpower. One reason being the easy and effortless way all their desires have been fulfilled since their childhood. Since they have not faced any hurdles in life, their willpower lies dormant. Thus, to increase willpower, it is important to face challenging situations.

Parents should let their children face challenges early on to raise their willpower and complete their assigned tasks, come what may. At the same time, these challenges need not be so hard that a child is unable to achieve the goal and loses confidence.

Along with relentless willpower, the power of discretion is also necessary to attain complete success. One should ascertain the pros and cons before undertaking them.

There is a human tendency to leave things unfinished as soon as one experiences obstacles. Hence, we need to face challenges with determination. Willpower develops only with courageous challenging encounters.

The line "**No matter what, DO IT**" can be used as a mantra to accomplish work when one experiences lethargy or are in a state of confusion. At the same time, one needs to find ways to complete the task, despite setbacks.

Tasks may be trivial or boring. We may have a hundred reasons for not doing them. Yet, if we manage to complete them successfully, it is an indication of relentless willpower.

Here's a short story of two friends desirous of losing weight. Both friends decided to lose 10 kilos in 4 months. One of them used his willpower and started regular exercises. He experienced a lot of challenges while striving to achieve his goal. There were times when he didn't feel like exercising or woke up late. At other times, it was extremely cold, or he had to reach office early. But he used the mantra "**No matter what, I have to exercise today**" and consistently worked towards his goal.

The other friend was unnerved with the thought, "How will I reduce 10 kilos in just four months?" He gave a lot of excuses to himself, like, "I have a lot of work to complete today; I have guests this evening; I am tired; I am feeling unwell; the weather is too bad," and so on. After 2 to 3 weeks, his desire to lose weight fizzled out.

Four months later, the first friend, with his relentless willpower, achieved his goal of losing weight. But despite having the desire, the other friend failed due to a lack of willpower.

If we too decide to accomplish something and are facing resistance or challenges in reaching the desired goal, we can make use of the mantra, "No matter what, DO IT." We can start by experimenting with small tasks. For example, "Today, I have to meet this person," or "I have to send that email today even if it is late," or "I have to make a phone call to that person." Begin with these small tasks, which require 2 to 5 minutes.

After experimenting with such small activities, you will experience a surge in your willpower, and that will, in turn, motivate you to achieve more significant tasks.

It is always better to be habituated to accomplishing tasks rather than leaving them unattended or incomplete. And when you approach each task with this attitude, you would be filled with a surge of willpower. Eventually, you will find that all your decided tasks get finished on time.

Create a contemplation chart to mention the tasks that you have been avoiding or postponing, and mention the steps you will take to complete them.

No.	Work to be accomplished	Reasons you've been giving for not completing it?	How to do it?
1	Reading	No time	I will read at least one page daily.

8

BREAK LAZY HABITS
CEASE EXCUSES

Willpower is intrinsic energy that is present within all human beings. How one harnesses this energy is an individual choice.

It remains unutilized in many as laziness gains priority to the point that it may lead to one's downfall. Lethargy leads to a lack of willpower. It is like a favorite gift that most people love to wallow in.

For example, a lazy person is always late to work. One day, he decides to wake up early to reach office on time. But, the next day, when the alarm rings at 5, he's unable to get up. At this time, sleeping is like a gift for him. He is filled with lethargy and is unable to open his eyes. Hence, he ends up reaching late and searches for lame excuses, just to escape the blame.

Laziness is a bad habit and also gives rise to another one—that of making excuses. Excuses are made for trivial tasks too, and so subtly that it is not obvious. This can be harmful to ourselves as well as others.

People generally give three types of excuses—bad reasons, big reasons, and good reasons.

1. **Bad Reasons:** These are lame excuses that reveal we are lazy. A person asked his cook, "What's on the menu today?"

Cook, "I am cooking fish today."

The master replied, "Fine. Just wash the fish thoroughly."

The cook quickly said, "The fish was already in water; what's the need to wash it?"

Listening to bad reasons like these, it is clear they are lame excuses.

2. **Big Reasons:** This involves using a big situation as an excuse, "I will complete this task in the New Year," "I will start this task after this festival," and so on. Accomplishing tasks is quite easy, but people who like shirking work use such excuses for non-performance.

3. **Good Reasons:** These reasons may not be considered as excuses, but if pondered over deeply, they prove to be excuses.

A father said to his son, "Son, please turn off the lights."

Son, "Dad, just close your eyes and imagine that the lights are off."

The father again, "Just peep outside and check whether it's raining."

Son, "Dad, our cat is underneath your bed. She just came in from outside. Touch her fur, and you will know whether it's raining or not."

The father is exasperated, "Close the door, please!"

Son, "Why should I do all the jobs? Why don't you do some yourself?"

The above conversation was a joke of how logical excuses can sound. Nobody can find any problems with these, but at the end of the day, they are just excuses!

People who are well-versed at giving excuses always leave tasks incomplete due to which they experience low confidence and self-esteem. This, in turn, leads to a lack of willpower.

Before making excuses, we need to ask ourselves, "Is the excuse that I am making up genuine and justified? Or does it merely sound logical? Or is it my laziness?" After such introspection, we will realize that we need to train ourselves.

Henceforth, whenever we make excuses, we should remind ourselves, **"No excuse, please!"** This line can be used as a mantra. We can scrutinize all the junctures in our daily routine, where we are tangled up with excuses.

Here are some examples: You want to complete a task today, but the mind says, "Not today." At such times, remind yourself, "No excuse, please!" You want to exercise, but your body is a little tired; tell yourself, "No excuse, please!" Or you want to meditate but you are feeling bored; use this mantra and get going.

In this way, we will be free of excuses and can complete our tasks on time.

To this mantra, we can add the understanding that our mind may create multiple excuses, but until the task does not attain completion, the work remains unfinished. The formula is **Laziness + Excuses = Incomplete Work**. Hence, instead of making excuses, we should decide to complete the task.

If dishes need to be cleaned in the evening, we may postpone it due to laziness. Instead, we should start cleaning them right away. If we have to message someone for a meeting, we should send it immediately. Doing these small tasks right away will boost our willpower.

By now, we must have realized the importance of willpower and would like to harness and develop it. To harness willpower, it is mandatory to follow these steps.

We should inspire ourselves with the advantages of being active so that the mind, intellect, and body supports us.

A servant is instructed to clean up the room.

He answers, "Let me have breakfast first."

On receiving a reminder, he says, "Let me take a nap first."

After a while, he says, "I will clean up the refrigerator first."

This indicates that the servant likes to complete his favorite tasks first.

The human body is generally programmed to complete favorite tasks first. But if we learn to complete the "first task first," then we shall be released of our lethargy and will cease our excuses.

List down the tasks that you've been postponing for a while and analyze them, as shown in the chart below. Eventually, you will see all your tasks getting completed.		
Tasks	Reasons for not completing the tasks Reason: Good-Big-Bad	How can it be accomplished?
Updating the bank account passbook	After Diwali	I can request someone else to help me with it.

9

STRENGTHENING WILLPOWER
CHALLENGE YOURSELF WITH A WORTHY GOAL

People experience dilemmas when they have no clear goal in their life. They feel lost when there is no clarity about the purpose of their life. This dual state of mind leads to the weakening of their willpower.

The life of a person without a goal resembles a horse without reins, running helter-skelter. He is unable to direct his mental and physical energy. He wastes time in trivial matters, thus delaying his success. Hence, possessing a clear goal should be of utmost priority.

When we decide an aim in life, all our thoughts get aligned in that direction. We experience a spurt in our willpower to achieve that aim. Our morale is used in the right manner too.

But this is possible only when we remember our goal at all times. For this to happen, it's necessary to write it down. When we write down our goal, we can observe it daily, feel, and live with it. We experience a spurt in our willpower as we start seeing it before our eyes and living with it.

Consider two people, each with their own goal. The first person writes down his goal everywhere—in his diary, on the mirror, on the whiteboard, as wallpapers on his mobile, laptop, etc.

He talks to other people about his goal. They, too, provide him guidance and encouragement. In this way, his willpower increases, and his desire to achieve his goal intensifies.

The other person also sets an aim. But his aim is just limited to his thoughts. After a few days, he forgets that he had set an aim for himself. He slides back to his old set patterns, and his willpower to achieve his aim drops down.

Dedication towards our goal fuels our willpower.

If you experience an ebb in your willpower despite setting a goal, then you can look up to your idol, your role model. In case you do not have an idol, then it is time to have one!

Everyone must have an idol in life. An idol is someone who is successful in all facets of life. You feel inspired to proceed towards your goal after seeing and listening to such a person. Your idol could be anyone—your parents, friends, boss, teacher, neighbor, or any renowned personality you have seen or read about and felt inspired.

For example, if someone wants to be a cricketer, then they can choose a cricketer as their role model. They can paste pictures of their idol in their room or diary. They should think about him, observe his playing style in detail, note his body language, watch his interviews, read his biography, etc.

Similarly, we can choose our idol according to our goals and start thinking about his or her qualities. We should try to feel those qualities within ourselves. When we begin contemplating about our idol, our willpower and qualities rise.

If we are in a dilemma about choosing our idol, then we can start reading biographies of successful leaders from any field. When we read such biographies, we will get to know about the adversities they had to face and the way they achieved their aim despite those challenges. Such reading intensifies our desire to accomplish something. Inspirational books spur our willingness to lead an exalted way of life. Motivational movies and songs also help us in this direction.

Having a goal and making someone a motivational force in our life helps raise our willpower.

Write down your aims; also mention how intensely you wish to achieve it and how you will remind yourself about it.		
Aim in Life	Desire to Achieve (on the scale of 1 – 10)	Where would you write your aim, and who would be your idol?
To be a Teacher	1, 2, 3, 4, 5, 6, 7, 8, 9, 10	On the Mirror, On the whiteboard, APJ Abdul Kalam
Scoring 85% in the exams		
To work for a multinational company		

10

BOOST YOUR WILLPOWER TO LIVE
INCREASE POSITIVITY

Some people have achieved insurmountable goals that will be considered impossible by others. This has been possible due to their immense willpower.

One such person, who achieved such unbeatable success, was Károly Takács. Károly was a soldier in the Hungarian army and a fervent patriot, besides being an excellent pistol shooter.

In 1938, Hungary desperately wanted to win an Olympic gold medal. During the Hungarian National Games, Károly won gold medals and fueled Hungarian hopes of winning gold in the 1940 Olympics.

Destiny had other plans, though. During an army training, a grenade burst in Károly's right hand (which he used for aiming), and it had to be amputated. But he faced this situation with immense courage and willpower.

He then began training with his left hand. A few months later, he returned to the limelight at the 1939 Hungarian National Games. His wish to perform in the Olympics surprised everyone, and he was granted permission to participate.

He miraculously won the gold medal! People were baffled. How was this possible? He was unable to write with his left hand a year back. How could he have trained this hand to shoot and achieve a gold medal?

Károly managed this impossible feat because of his immense willpower. Each one of us has the latent energy of willpower within us. But the important question that we need to ask ourselves is – do we utilize this energy? Most people find such situations very challenging, and to add to it, disability is a big challenge in itself. Most people even lose their hope of living, but Károly succeeded.

A hospital had two patients suffering from the same illness. The doctor told them that their chances of survival were very less. Both of them started experiencing different thoughts in their minds.

The first patient thought, "I won't survive; the doctor has given up on me. There is no point in living now. This disease will kill me, anyway."

The second patient thought, "Whatever the doctor may have to say, I am going to live. I have to do a lot of good for people. God is with me, and he has blessed me."

From these thoughts, we can very well infer what would have occurred. The first patient could not overpower his disease and did not survive. The second patient overcame his illness and lived a healthy life, also helping others improve their lives.

Both the patients faced the same situation. Yet the results were different as both had varying levels of willpower. The one who had an intense wish to live was filled with positive thoughts. He automatically experienced a surge in his desire to live. The other was full of negativity; he lost his hope and desire to live.

Willpower is dependent on a person's thoughts. A person with positive thoughts feels empowered to live. A person with negative thoughts experiences a lag in his willpower.

People face various life situations: a close one is down with a terminal disease, someone suffers a breakup, another fails his exams, someone loses her job, someone commits a grave mistake and feels weighed down by the guilt. In such situations, the mind is full of negative thoughts, and the person eventually loses his desire to live.

Many a time, we feel, "This situation is making me unhappy. If it were not for this situation, I would have been happy." But the truth is that situations, by themselves, are not responsible for our unhappiness. Instead, the thoughts that occur after these incidents are responsible for our sorrow. These thoughts are responsible for weakening our willpower.

To increase our desire to live, we should be positive at all times and learn to love ourselves. Love holds power to revive one's hope, can turn negative thinking to positive, a weak person to a strong one, and an unhealthy person to a healthy one.

Psychiatrists, too, implore people who are depressed and unhappy to find a purpose for living. They ask them to be positive and to love themselves.

Imagine the hopelessness one may feel when he decides to commit suicide. Such a situation arises only when one hates oneself for some reason. Hence, it is necessary to love ourselves first because the day we stop loving ourselves, we lose our desire to live.

Conclusively, harboring positive thoughts and loving ourselves will increase our willpower. No adverse situation will have the power to weaken us and, instead, will only strengthen and increase our willpower.

Write down the positive thoughts that you will affirm to yourself to counter vulnerable situations.	
Weak Willpower	**Positive thoughts to strength willpower**
Suicidal thoughts	I love myself, and this situation has come to help me progress in my life.

11

AUGMENTING WILLPOWER
TECHNIQUES TO STRENGTHEN WILLPOWER

Every human being is gifted with the quality of willpower in varied amounts right from childhood. This variation depends on one's surroundings, habits, and practice.

Children should be given an opportunity to develop this quality within themselves right from childhood. We may feel, what's the point? But it is important to understand that mental growth takes place in early childhood. If children are trained right from the beginning, it will boost their inner power of resoluteness.

Mostly, physical strength is considered important. But to achieve any goal, inner strength is also necessary. Helen Keller, Nick Vujicic, Jessica Cox are some examples of physically challenged people, who turned their weakness into strength with their willpower and have become a source of inspiration for many.

Following are four techniques to help us increase our willpower and inner strength.

1.　Slowly increase resoluteness

We should start by making small resolutions as fulfilling them helps boost our confidence, which further helps to increase willpower and inner strength.

Many a time, we commit the mistake of setting a big goal and then are unable to achieve it. Consequently, we start losing willpower and our morale. Big aims require a lot of inner strength, which we may not possess at the outset. Due to this, we may lose our confidence, eventually resulting in failure.

> For example, a person who has never done exercises, one day decides, "I will do exercises for an hour every day." In the beginning, he is very enthusiastic and exercises regularly. But as time progresses, he develops self-doubt and feels, "I may not be able to continue this for the whole year."
>
> It is of utmost importance for one to feel deep within that he will be able to achieve his goal. Only then will he be able to see the results. Hence setting smaller goals and achieving them becomes crucial.
>
> Hence, when the same person decides, "I will practice *Pranayam* for 10 minutes every day and gradually increase my time," now there is a possibility that his mind will agree to do this for 10 minutes daily. Doing exercises for 10 minutes is more achievable compared to 60 minutes. His mind is agreeable to achieve this small goal as it is easier.

In this way, small steps help one boost his morale. This gives a message to the subconscious mind, and it starts believing in one's ability to achieve goals.

Begin with small resolutions and complete them. This will increase willpower and resoluteness. Here are some examples:

a) If you want to wake up early, then begin with a resolve to wake up five minutes earlier than your usual time. Try this experiment for a week. In the next week, try waking up five minutes earlier than the previous week; repeat the same the following week. In this manner, there will be a time when you will be able to wake up at the time you had decided.

b) If you want to drink four bottles of water every day, begin with one initially. After a week, add another bottle; and then after yet another week, add one more. Begin with small steps and gradually increase.

c) If you want to reduce the intake of sugar or salt in your diet, begin by reducing a pinch first. Your taste buds will slowly get used to eating less sugary and bland foods, and you will easily work towards attaining good health.

With these small successful resolves, the subconscious mind will receive a new message that you are capable of achieving the goals you decide. This will further help eliminate habits that reduce your willpower.

2. Working against our desire

Each one of us desires that things happen our way and find it difficult to tolerate obstructions. So, when the mind becomes a slave of desires, our willpower starts diminishing.

At such times, working against our desires helps us. When we deliberately work against our desires, it helps fuel our inner determination.

Feeble mental strength may result due to weak willpower. At such times we can become aware of our small desires and work against them.

Here are some examples:

- Sometimes, decide and miss the daily series that you watch on television sometimes. When you are eagerly watching a cricket match, try switching off your TV during the last over.
- If you are hungry and feel like feasting on some fast food like *samosas*, or *chaat*, etc., you can instead have some fruit. Fruit will not just satisfy your hunger but will also work against your desire to eat junk food.

3. Make small promises to oneself

We can make small promises to ourselves and complete them. This is another useful technique to increase our willpower.

- For example, promise yourself, "Today for a while, I will only listen to the other person." This will not just increase your willpower, but also increase your concentration.
- While listening to a song, promise, "More than the lyrics, today I will pay attention to the background score, the instruments used, and its melody." This will help increase your awareness.
- You can decide, "Today I am going to notice all red objects around me." Check all the rooms, venture outside. In this way, you can choose different colors on different days and practice this exercise for a couple of minutes. It will increase your observation besides your willpower.

While practicing the above exercises, if you experience some other desire, ignore it and just complete the task you have assigned yourself.

Accomplishing these small promises sends a new signal to our subconscious mind that we are committed. All this while, we have been completing some tasks and might have missed some; hence the subconscious mind has always been confused. It's important to give a new signal to the subconscious mind. Hence, from today, resolve to keep your promises, so as to increase your willpower.

4. Using concentration to strengthen willpower

Concentration is yet another effective way to increase willpower. When one concentrates, his mind and full attention are centered on one thing.

An unruly, frantic mind and uncontrollable senses impede willpower. Hence it is important to increase concentration. When our thoughts, actions, feelings, and words are unified in a chosen direction, it helps to strengthen our willpower and achieve our goal.

Try the following experiments to improve your concentration.

a) Twine the fingers of both your hands with each other for 5 minutes. Do not open them till the allotted time is complete.

Your mind will keep prodding you to untwine your fingers at times, but you have to remain steadfast.

b) Watch the clock continuously for a minute with a steady mind till it completes one turn. This technique helps concentrate your mind for a few minutes.

c) To increase your concentration, you can also practice **Tratak meditation.** Instructions are as follows:

1. Select a quiet room for yourself.
2. Get a burning candle or oil lamp. If it's not possible to use a lighted candle, you can download a video of a lit candle.
3. Place the candle or lamp at a hand's length right in front of your eyes.
4. Set a timer for 10 to 15 minutes.
5. Keep a wet towel handy if you feel sleepy.
6. Close your eyes and sit in a meditative posture.
7. Breathe in and out slowly three times.
8. Open your eyes and concentrate your gaze on the wick of the candle.
9. Do not blink your eyes while gazing at the flame. Initially, you may blink a few times, but gradually, this shall reduce. The aim is not to increase the time interval, but to focus.
10. Even if you blink your eyes, do not worry, concentrate again on the wick of the candle.
11. Now, close your eyes and try to see the candle in your mind's eye.
12. If you feel sleepy, wipe your face with the towel, or you may stand for a while and sit again.
13. When the timer goes off, sit with your eyes closed for a while. Open your eyes slowly and get up.

These small techniques will help train the mind so that we can achieve big miracles in our life with the help of our augmented willpower and inner strength.

As we come to the end of this book, here's another contemplation chart that comes handy. Contemplate and write down the important points that you have gathered from this book. You can create a tabular chart as below and work on one technique every week.

	Contemplation Chart
No.	Write the important points you have gathered from this book.
1.	Using the raised-hand "NO" gesture, say, "I am not going to indulge in this." It will help in attaining control over the senses.
2.	

As you start practicing each technique, you will notice a change in your perspective towards life. This will boost your confidence and willpower, not only leading you towards success, but also helping you stay there.

• • •

You can mail your opinion or feedback on this book to: books.feedback@tejgyan.org

About Sirshree

Sirshree's spiritual quest, which began during his childhood, led him on a journey through various schools of philosophy and meditation practices. He studied a wide range of literature on mind science and spirituality. After a long period of deep contemplation on the truth of life, his quest culminated in attaining the ultimate truth.

Sirshree espouses, "All spiritual paths that lead to the truth begin differently but culminate at the same point – Understanding. This understanding is complete in itself. Listening to this understanding is enough to attain the Truth." Over the last two decades, he has dedicated his life to raise mass consciousness.

Sirshree has delivered more than 4000 discourses that throw light on this understanding. He has designed a system for wisdom, which makes it accessible to all. This system has inspired people from all walks of life to progress on their journey of the Truth. Thousands of seekers join in a virtual prayer for World Peace and Global Healing daily at 9:09 am and 9:09 pm.

About Tej Gyan Foundation

Tej Gyan Foundation is a non-profit organization founded on the teachings of Sirshree. The Foundation disseminates Tejgyan – the wisdom that guides one from self-development to Self-realization, leading towards Self-stabilization.

The Foundation's system for imparting wisdom has been assessed by international quality auditors and accredited with the ISO 9001:2015 certification. This wisdom has been presented in a simple, systematic, and practically applicable form that makes it accessible to people from all walks of life, regardless of religion, caste, social strata, country, or belief system.

The Foundation has centers in more than 400 cities and towns across India and other countries. The mission of Tej Gyan Foundation is to create a highly evolved society by leading seekers from negative thoughts to positive thoughts and further, from positive thoughts to Happy thoughts. A 'Happy thought' is the auspicious thought of being free from all thoughts, leading to the state of supreme bliss beyond thoughts.

If you seek such wisdom that leads you beyond mere knowledge, dissolves all problems, frees you from all limiting beliefs, reveals the true nature of divinity, and establishes you in the ultimate truth, then it is time to discover Tejgyan; it is time to rise above the mundane knowledge of words and experience Tejgyan!

The MahaAasmani Magic of Awakening Retreat

Self-development to Self-realization towards Self-stabilization

Do you wish to experience unconditional happiness that is not dependent on any reason? Happiness that is permanent and only increases with time? Do you wish to experience love, peace, self-belief, harmony in relationships, prosperity, and true contentment? Do you wish to progress in all facets of your life, viz. physical, mental, social, financial, and spiritual?

If you seek answers to these questions and are thirsty for the ultimate truth, then you are welcome to participate in the MahaAasmani Magic of Awakening retreat organized by Tej Gyan Foundation. This is the Foundation's flagship retreat based on the teachings of Sirshree.

The purpose of this retreat

The purpose of this retreat is that every human being should:

- Discover the answer to "Who am I" and "Why am I?" through direct experience and be established in ultimate bliss.

- Learn the art of living in the present, free from the burden of the past and the anxiety of the future.

- Acquire practical tools to help quieten the chattering mind and dissolve problems.

- Discover missing links in the practices of Meditation (*Dhyana*), Action (*Karma*), Wisdom (*Gyana*), and Devotion (*Bhakti*).

About Books by Sirshree

Sirshree's published work includes more than 150 book titles, some of which have been translated into more than 10 languages. His literature provides a profound reading on various topics of practical living and unravels the missing links in karma, wisdom, devotion, meditation, and consciousness.

His books have been published by leading publishing houses like Penguin, Hay House, Bloomsbury, Wisdom Tree, Jaico, etc. "The Source" book series, authored by Sirshree, has sold over 10 million copies. Various luminaries and celebrities like His Holiness the Dalai Lama, publishers Mr. Reid Tracy, Ms. Tami Simon and Yoga Master Dr. B. K. S. Iyengar have released Sirshree's books and lauded his work.

The Source
Attain Both, Inner Peace
and Worldly success

Awaken the Power of Faith
Discover the 7 Principles of the
Highest Power of the Universe

To order books authored by Sirshree, login to:
www.gethappythoughts.org
For further details, call: +91 9011013210

Tej Gyan Foundation – Contact details

Registered Office:
Happy Thoughts Building, Vikrant Complex, Near Tapovan Mandir, Pimpri, Pune 411017, INDIA. Contact: +91 20-27411240, +91 20-27412576

MaNaN Ashram:
Survey No. 43, Sanas Nagar, Nandoshi Gaon, Kirkatwadi Phata, Off Sinhagad Road, Taluka Haveli, Pune district - 411024, INDIA. Contact: +91 992100 8060.

WORLD PEACE PRAYER

Divine Light of Love, Bliss, and Peace is Showering;

The Golden Light of Higher Consciousness is Rising;

All negativity on Earth is Dissolving;

Everyone is in Peace and Blissfully Shining;

O God, Gratitude for Everything!

Members of Tej Gyan Foundation have been offering this impersonal mass prayer for many years. Those who are happy can offer this prayer. Those feeling low or suffering from illness can receive healing with this prayer.

If you are feeling troubled or sick, please sit to receive the healing effect of this prayer. Visualize that the divine white healing light is being showered on earth through the prayers of thousands and is also reaching you, bringing you peace and good health. You can dwell in this feeling for some time and then offer your gratitude to those offering the prayer.

A Humble Appeal

More than a million peace lovers pray for World Peace and Global Healing every morning and evening at 9:09. Also, a prayer (in Hindi) to elevate consciousness is webcast every day on YouTube at 3:30 pm and 9:00 pm IST. Please participate in this noble endeavor.

www.ingramcontent.com/pod-product-compliance
Lightning Source LLC
LaVergne TN
LVHW041551070526
838199LV00046B/1902